1776 And All That

PETER E. CHANDLER

DEDICATION

This book is dedicated to all those who suffer from
or have friends or family who suffer from Alzheimer's Disease.

Royalties from this edition will be donated to the Alzheimer's Society.

CONTENTS

ACKNOWLEDGMENTS

Illustrations have been provided royalty fee under the appropriate licenses from the following:
GoGraph https://www.gograph.com
FCIT https://etc.usf.edu/clipart/info
IStock https://www.istockphoto.com
(Including the flags on the cover of this book.)

The author would also like to thank the wife, the Penny and the wonderful Wikipedia - not that the wife and the Penny are not wonderful too!

COMPULSORY PREFACE

(THIS MEANS YOU)

"1066 and all that" (1) was a "Memorable History of England" comprising all the parts you can remember, including 103 Good Things, 5 Bad Kings and 2 Genuine Dates". It ends (Spoiler Alert!) after the Great War when America (2) became Top Nation and English history came to a full stop.

Now, despite America's undoubted success all empires come with an expiry date. Although Americans might not like this, the next Top Nation, The Peoples Republic of China, is growling impatiently in the wings. Who can doubt that after the unedifying shenanigans of the last American Presidential election the end is pretty much nigh.

Furthermore, as it is the four hundredth anniversary of Mayflower's arrival, it seems an appropriate time for a new "Memorable History" but this time of America. This small tract has been compiled in much the same way as a modern-day Tribute Band. It will steal as much as possible from the original and hope that no one notices that it is nowhere near as good. It will, of course, still comprise all the parts of American history you can remember but with slightly fewer Good Things, 5 Bad Presidents instead of Kings and 3 extra Genuine Dates (sorry). So here goes, a memorable history of America, "1766 and all that".

America's Cracked Liberty (Courtesy of FCIT).

1 HISTORY REPEATS ITSELF, REPEATS ITSELF

A brief word about dates

One of the biggest problems with history is that it has too many dates. This puts a lot of people off. The authors of the history of England "1066 and all that" appreciated this and much of its success can be attributed to the fact that they used only two Genuine Dates.

As this is a Memorable History of America more dates are needed. Not being as good as the original, 3 Genuine Dates and one Non-date have had to be added. Hopefully, this extravagant lack of discipline will not put too many people off.

On the other hand, this Memorable History will adhere to the Dominique Calendar convention (3) that history unfolds in the order in which things happen. Dominique was the inventor of the Calendar in what he called year zero (the Non-date). Subsequent years were marked AD (After Dominique) and prior events, marked BC (Before Calendar) and were counted backwards.

To give an example of how this works; American history began in 1492 AD. If we go back say 3000 years and drop in on the Meadowcroft family in a rock shelter 27 miles SW of what is now Pittsburgh (4) then that would be the year 1508 BC. This was long time ago and so it is called the Archaic Period of American history.

The problem is, that unlike Dominique, we now know how old the Earth really is and so Dominique's year zero was out by a staggering 4,540,000,003 years. Another reason why it is best to avoid dates altogether!

1

Doomed to make the same mistakes

Apparently the one thing that people never learn from is history. Churchill borrowing the idea from a musical genius called Santana (5) said it slightly differently; 'Those who fail to learn from history are doomed to repeat it.' Apart from viewers of daytime TV, nothing illustrates this better than empires. History is littered with them rising up, throwing their weight around for a bit and then falling. Even gibbons (6) understood this so why can't people? To remove any lingering doubt that this is true, a few empires are discussed below.

(Authors Note. This short digression is purely voluntary so please feel free to jump on to Chapter 2. I won't be offended. That you are still reading up to this point is good enough for me!)

Ancient Empires

The Egyptians lived along the river Nile and invented irrigation (the shaduf), paper (papyrus) and funny writing (hieroglyphs) (7). They were ruled over by Pharaohs who lived apart from the general population in large pyramids. Here they hoarded all sorts of treasure that they refused to pass onto their children. On the plus side they loved their mummies, adored cats and even allowed women to be Pharaohs. Cleopatra and her ass was the most famous one but another, named Hatshepsut, is credited as having invented eyeliner.

Home of the Pharaohs (Courtesy of FCIT)

As with all hereditary rulers there were bad Pharaohs and very bad ones. The bad ones used slaves to do all the heavy lifting but a very bad one (Ramses ll) enslaved a whole people, the Hebrews. Their story is told in the

Bible (Exodus aka "I'm Jewish get me out of here") and colourfully re-told in the documentary "Ten Commandments" where Moses (Charlton Heston) leads his people to freedom as Cecil B. DeMille (God) parts the waters of the Nile to let them through. Unfortunately, the Pharaohs became complacent and following military defeats and civil unrest (after all, the slaves had all the jobs), the Empire began to crumble. A Greek named Alexander was a great help in defeating the Persians and the Egyptians were so pleased that they made Alexander a god.

The two civilisations had a pleasant co-existence until Rome rose up and took over as Top Nation. Later Caesar and his general Mark Anthony both met Egypt's last Pharaoh, Cleopatra. Had she stuck to pyramids and left triangles well alone, things might have worked out better for her.

The Greek Empire got off to a really good start because they invented democracy. In fact, they invented lots of things: the arts (Tragedies), architecture (Parthenons) and most importantly fighting. The Greeks were known for their massive Phalanx and this helped the Greeks create a really large empire. They were also known to give their enemies gifts which gave rise to two contradictory expressions; "Don't look a gift horse in the mouth" and "Beware Greeks bearing gifts". History is sometimes very confusing.

The Trojan Horse (Courtesy of FCIT)

3

The Greek Empire was started by Philip ll but it was his son, Alexander, who greatly increased its size to dominate the ancient world. Alexander's teacher was Aristotle who was good at all kinds of sums (he was a Polymath). Later, Alexander made his school chums his Generals and they went on to win every battle until they ran out of people to fight. To quote the villain from "Die Hard" and to mis-quote Plutarch, "When Alexander saw the breadth of his domain, he wept for there were no more worlds to conquer."

Alexander was only 32 when he died (Skulduggery was the prime suspect). As he had not named an heir, his generals carved up the empire among themselves and Greek history came to a full stop.

The Romans had a lot of history before they became Top Nation. It was originally a Republic and run by a Senate of Senators. The Romans liked wars and became very good at them and there was no better military commander than Julius Caesar. Outside the Roman territories were many different tribes. They all had one thing in common namely eating garlic. Julius set about conquering them one by one and confiscating all their valuables. Because of the eating habits of the tribes and their terrible bad breath these battles became known as the Garlic Wars.

Caesar planned to bring all this pelf back to Rome and pay for lots of games for the people to play with, become very popular, kick out the Senators and then take over. Unfortunately, the Senate got wise to what Caesar was up to and ordered him to leave his army behind the Rubicon and come back to Rome to face the music. Julius stood looking at the Rubicon then muttering "anerriphtho kybos!" which is Greek for "let the die be cast", he crossed with his army. Now some pedants try to put the kybosh on the kybos by insisting that as Julius spoke Latin he would have said "Alea iacta est". Well, kybos or alea Julius rolled a six, won the civil war and became Dictator of Rome.

Cleopatra and her ass (Courtesy of GoGraph)

As icing on the cake, Cleopatra came to town for a visit and Julius was smitten and vice versa (Latin for vice versa). Of course, it was not going to end there. The Senators plotted and led by a brute of a man, stabbed Julius in the theatre. But the Senator's cunning plan to restore the Republic was not to be and instead the Roman Empire was born and extensively mined by Shakespeare for his Roman plays (8).

Shakespeare's Roman Plays in a Nutshell. Caesar was indeed popular with the masses who became enraged that a small, political elite had murdered their Caesar. Antony, was about to capitalise on this but to his chagrin, found that Caesar had named his grandnephew Gaius Octavius his sole heir. So they joined forces and made another civil war against Brutus and his followers defeating them at Philippi. Meanwhile, Mark Antony married Caesar's lover, Cleopatra, intent on using her fabulous wealth from Egypt to take Rome. So a third civil war broke out between Antony and Cleopatra against Octavian. This culminated in Octavians's victory at Actium. He made himself the first Roman emperor but changed his name to Caesar Augustus. Here Cleopatra's triangle finally ended. Anthony stabbed himself and Cleopatra was bitten by her ass.

Shakespeare eventually gave up on Roman history. It was left to I Claudius to continue the story of his family squabbles and poisonings, brutal murders, madness and finally, of course, Nero playing with matches and fiddling while Rome burned. Although all this history was a bit on the bloody side it should be remembered that, as the documentary "The Life of Brian" reveals, the Romans did quite a lot for us.

After the fall of Rome, tallow production (9) stopped and the lights went out all over Europe. This was called the Dark Ages. When the lights came back on Europeans had reached their Middle Age and so started empire building again before it was too late. They did this with even more skulduggery and even nastier nastiness. This became a bit of a trademark of European empires as we will see below.

Modern Empires

In modern times, the Germans were first to put an Imperial towel on the symbolic deckchair with their **Holy Roman Empire** (the German 1st Reich). As their emperor was crowned by the Pope it had to be a Catholic empire. Catholic empires used religion as a weapon to convert and control people. Woe betide anyone who did not willingly convert especially Puritans, Jews, Muslims, Aztecs and anyone else they did not like and could accuse of heresy. It came to an abrupt end after Napoleon's victory at Austerlitz.

The **Spanish Empire**, was another Catholic one which began by colonising half of North and South America. It became the dominant naval power until the British Queen Elizabeth the Thirst gave her Privateers (aka Pirates) carte blanche to sink Spanish ships and steal all their gold and wine. Sir Francis Drake also raided Spanish ports, set fire to their ships and singed King Phillip's beard. Phillip was furious as it had taken him a long time to grow one. He sent an Armada to crush the English once and for all.

This time Drake was furious as he was in the middle of a game of bowls at the time. It was a big mistake to annoy Sir Francis and that was the end of the Spanish navy.

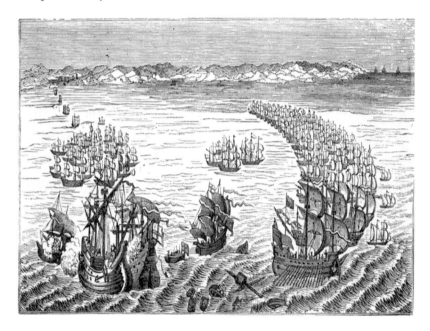

Drake Sets Off to Bowl Some Googlies into the Spanish Armada
(Courtesy of IStock)

The **French Empire** was built by a Corse little corporal. Actually, Napoleon had made himself a General but he was indeed only 5' 2". Napoleon was a nasty, little man who made everyone drive on the wrong side of the road. Yes, driving on the right is wrong. Most people are right handed so had to ride on the left so that their sword arm was free if needed. This is the same reason why a castle's staircases go up clockwise. As Napoleon conquered countries he made people move over to the wrong side to let him pass.

Meanwhile, Spain had built some more ships and joined the French fleet at Trafalgar. Together they outnumbered the British so had a huge advantage when the fighting started. Nelson, even with only one eye, could see the problem so advanced his fleet in an arrow formation to pierce through the centre of the enemy line. It was a brave tactic as the British ships came under heavy fire which they could not return until they had broken through. But when they did the enemy ships went down like ninepins. Victory for Nelson and another English bowler saved the day on a very sticky wicket (10). This cricketing metaphor is very appropriate as Nelson was famous for bowling bouncers. His gunners often skimmed cannon balls off the water for much greater effect. This technique was used again by the British in World War 2 when bombing the damn Germans.

On land, after his victory at Austerlitz, Napoleon was on a high (but only when sitting on his horse, Marshal Neigh).

Napoleon on his horse Marshal Neigh (Courtesy of FCIT)

Unfortunately, Napoleon was no metallurgist and led a winter attack on the Russians. A big mistake as his soldier's buttons were made of tin which, at low temperatures, undergo a phase change and disintegrate. Even Napoleon could not get his soldiers to fight with their trousers round their ankles and so they hopped a Heroic Retreat from Moscow. Undeterred, he then attacked the British. Wellington, wearing his famous boots, was waiting for Napoleon in a muddy field called Belgium and it was here that Napoleon met his Waterloo.

One interesting thing about Napoleon's rule was the introduction of the Blocus Continental (Continental Blockade) against the English. As we will see this tactic was used again in World War 2 and more recently, it is being threatened by the Franco-German Empire (aka the EU) during Brexit trade talks (see below).

The next **German Empire** (the 2nd Reich) came to a sticky end after the Great War (see later). Yet another German Empire, the 3rd Reich, rose up after the Great Depression and was by any measure the nastiest Empire in the list. While it was supposed to last for a thousand years it was, fortunately, put down within a decade but at a very heavy cost. The German leader was A Dolf Hitler. If you thought that Egypt's treatment of the Hebrews was bad A Dolf went much, much further and tried to exterminate the entire Jewish race. By the end of the war the Germans had murdered 6 million of them (11).

After two consecutive world wars you would have thought that Europeans, especially the Germans and the French, would have had enough of Empires but no, they just refused to learn from history. A German born Frenchman, Valerie G'reat d'Isdain drew up yet another long-winded treaty, not in Paris this time but in the rather dull, Dutch city of Maastricht. The Maastricht Treaty created the European Union as a putative State, now known as "The 27 United States of Europe". To show how grand they were, the EU and its institutions appointed not one but six presidents. Coincidentally they come from the two member States who make all the decisions with two from the de facto Capital, Brussels. Currently they are:

German: Merkel (Presidency of Council)
German: Ursula von der Leyen (President, European Commission)
German: Klaus-Heiner Lehne (President European Court of Auditors)
French: Christine Legarde (President of the European Central Bank)
Belgian: Michel (President of the European Council)
Belgian: Koen Lenaerts (President of the Court of Injustice)

There is a European Parliament and a European Court of inJustice (ECiJ) but no democratic Constitution or real democratic mandate. Essentially, the
leaders of Germany and France decide what is best for them and then bully/bribe everyone else to agree. The ECiJ prosecutes anyone who does not do what they are told especially the British and any passing American Corporation.

The English became fed up with yet another Franco-German set-up that kept telling them what to do and taking all their money and fish. In fact, the EU were taking so many fish that there was a danger there would be none left for the British to have their famous fish and chips! The British thus voted for Brexit (12).

As this was not what France and Germany wanted, the EU set out to punish the British and impose a Suzerainty Treaty (13) and another Blocus. Continental. Interestingly, after Naploleon's Blocus, the loss of British trade hit the economies of France and its allies so they began to ignore it, weakening Napoleon's coalition.

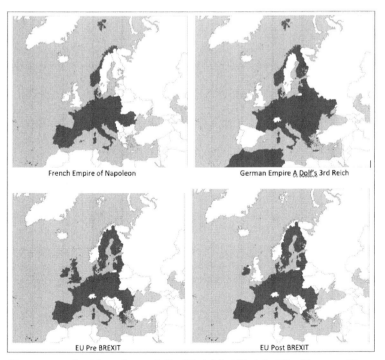

Europe under Napoleon, A Dolf's Third Reich. The Franco-German EU - Pre-Brexit and the EU - Post Brexit restoring the UK's Independence.

Europe never learns from history. Why despots and tyrants still think that it is a good idea to build an empire knowing they will come to a sticky end is puzzling. For historians, it is proof positive that history repeats itself and we shall see, many of the elements of these past empires appear again and again in the following memorable history of America.

2 THE TIME BEFORE AMERICAN HISTORY BEGAN

As everybody knows, American history began in 1492 when Christopher Columbus discovered it. This obviously came as a bit of a surprise to the indigenous population of Native Americans, who had been living there for many thousands of years. So too to the Vikings who had already discovered it but because they were renowned for eating hallucinogenic mushrooms and drinking massive amounts of alcohol, no one believed them.

So, instead of having to start off American history much earlier and spoil a good story, historians played their usual trick of calling everything before 1492 "pre-history" so that it could be ignored. This was perfectly acceptable since in 1492 the "natives" were actually Indians and not Americans. Columbus always insisted that his voyages had taken him to the Indies, the East Indies that is.

Turtle Island

Strangely, the "natives" had no idea who the Indians were nor indeed how to play cricket. If anyone had bothered to ask them they would have said they were natives of Turtle Island.

Now, the idea that the Earth was carried on the back of a giant turtle is not limited to Terry Pratchett's Discworld series (14). The illustration below of the "Hindu Earth" (15) is one of many cultural examples of this belief. Native Americans, such as the Iroquois, believed that the Earth was created by soil piled on the back of a great sea turtle until it was carrying the entire world. Many North America tribes referred to the continent as Turtle

Island.

The world on the back of a giant turtle
(Courtesy of GoGraph)

The Peoples of Turtle Island

Today, 574 Native American tribes have legal recognition. It is impossible to give an accurate figure for how many millions there were in 1492. One thing was certain, there were soon going to be a lot, lot less of them. Like modern day America there were distinct cultural differences between the east and west coasts and those who frequented the great plains of middle America. Oddly, one of the main distinguishing features was their houses.

The cultural areas of the Native Americans
(Courtesy of GoGraph)

The East Coast

The Northeast was the home of the famous wigwam. This was a round building made from logs, covered with bark and colourfully decorated. The Algonquin were the most peaceful of the tribes and they included the Wampanoag whose famous son, Squanto would, as we shall see later, be a godsend to the Pilgrim Fathers. Other tribes such as the Ikeans made their wigwams by assembling a wooden frame and covering it with hide. When they moved, the hide was rolled up and taken with them. The frame stayed so when they returned they simply unrolled the original covering and placed it back on the frame. Easy to assemble flatpack was born.

In the Southeast people were mainly farmers and included the Choctaw, Chickasaw, Seminole, Creek and Cherokee people. They imbibed a coffee like drink called Cassina made from holly leaves. Note, if you drank too much of it, it lived up to its Latin name, Ilex vomitoria!

Well it looked like coffee! (Courtesy of GoGraph)

Uniquely, amongst the Native Americans, they embraced the language, religion and customs of the white settlers and became known as the "Five Civilized Tribes." Needless to say, this willingness to embrace multiculturalism did not help them one jot in the end.

Muddle America

In the early days, Muddle America was much more diverse than it is now. The Shoshone of the Great Basin were always on the move in their wikiups, an early form of Winnebago. On the other hand, the Plateau people had three different homes. A pleasant summer residence, a temporary one for when they were out doing their hunting and gathering and a winter one which was a, Pythonesque "pit int' middle o' road". Finally, down on the Plains where the buffalo roamed, the home of choice for the Crow, Blackfeet, Cheyenne, Comanche and Arapaho were cone-shaped, tee-pees. These tribes also wore elaborately feathered war bonnets and it was these "Indians" that became the stuff of Western legend.

War Bonnet (Courtesy of GoGraph)

The West Coast

The Northwest had a mild climate so tribes such as the Tlingit and Nootka lived in settlements and became skilled in various arts and crafts. They also went in for the beach house look and built large structures from cedar planks.

In the Southwest the Navajo boasted two homes, one for the desert and one for the mountains. These were called hogans and made from poles covered with mud and bark. There were also the Pueblo Indians who invented apartment living and built multi-story brick pueblos in local rock faces and on mesas. As they had not invented lifts they had to use a series of ladders to get to the upper floors but once there a corridor linked to everyone's front door. Finally, there were the fearlessly aggressive Apache. In fact, their name was what other tribes called them meaning "enemy". They much preferred this appellation to their real name of Nde which rather boringly just meant Nde. They also lived in Wickiups but these were made by bending over young trees to make a frame and then covering them with hides. They were not very spacious but could be dismantled quickly leaving no trace that they were ever there. Presumably it was Apache braves who used their expertise in tree bending to help Painless Potter (aka Bob Hope) become detached from his boots in Paleface.

Even back then, California was a popular place to live with an estimated 300,000 people. More than any other cultural area. They organized themselves into small, family-based bands of hunter-gatherers and were generally very peaceful. Their slogan "Peace and Love, Peace and Love" was later adopted by the 5th best drummer in the Beatles, Ringo Starr.

3 COLONIAL AMERICA

Christopher Columbus

When Columbus announced his plan people thought him quite mad. Washington put it quite succinctly. "Sailing east to get to China indeed. He'll just fall off the edge if he goes that way!" No, it was not George but Irving Washington, the master storyteller of "Rip Van Winkle" fame. His "Life and Voyages of Christopher Columbus" was probably responsible for the flat earth myth. Indeed, no educated person of Columbus's time believed in a flat earth. On the other hand, Columbus had no idea how big the Earth was. He had been for a drink with fellow countryman Paolo Toscanelli and they got talking. By happenstance Paolo was a bit of a cartographer and so he drew out the westerly route to India on the back of a napkin. It was down to the Azores and then a quick island hop across the Atlantic and there would be India.

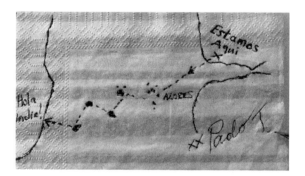

Toscanelli's Napkin Map to India © Chandler

England and the Persecution of the Puritans

When the much married, Henry VIII split from Rome and invented the Church of England, a few of the old Roman Catholic practices remained. While some (Puritans) thought that he had gone far enough others (the Purer, Puritans) wanted to purify the new church of all the old ways. Unfortunately, the next dynasty of English kings, the Stuarts, liked the old ways and since they ruled by Divine Right everyone had to follow them and woe betide anyone who didn't. Now some Puritans, like the Vicar of Bray (16), adopted a laissez-faire attitude to religion so just went with the flow. The more radical separatists wanted to do their own thing and were not going to take being told what to do lying down. In fact many of them got up, got into ships and sailed off to America where they could create a purely, pure, puritan way of life. The State of Massachusetts was especially selective as to which Puritans they let in.

The Puritans that stayed behind in England soon became a force to be reckoned with and the reckoning came when the second Stuart King, Charles completely lost his head. The English now became a sort of Republic but their puritan leader, Oliver "Roundhead" Cromwell, just made everyone miserable. Nobody was allowed to have any fun and he even banned Christmas. Understandably, the monarchy was soon restored but the new Stuart Kings had learnt nothing from history and became Catholics. They were then overthrown and replaced with a nice Puritan Dutch couple. To keep future rulers in their place a Bill of Rights was drawn up. A hundred years later the Americans would follow suit.

The Pilgrim Fathers

When the English separatists arrived in America they called themselves the "Old Comers". It was not until two hundred years later, at the bicentennial celebration of their arrival, that the legendary phrase "Pilgrim Fathers" was used. Apart from not being The Pilgrim Fathers, three other legends were created:

1. Religious Persecution. They were not escaping religious persecution. While it is true that the various puritan sects had been persecuted in England the Pilgrim Fathers had already escaped to the safety of Holland where they were living with complete religious freedom. The real problem was that their children were losing their Englishness and picking up far too many disgusting habits from the "more relaxed" Dutch. That is why they set off for America.

2. They Set Sail from Plymouth. No, they set sail from Southampton. The Pilgrims had hired one ship, the Mayflower in Gravesend and bought a second from the Dutch. The plan was for everyone to meet up in Southampton, provision the two ships and from there set sail to America.

Now the ship they bought in Holland had a big sign on it saying "Lekkende Bodem". The seller translated this into English as "Speed Well". In a sense this was quite accurate as when they put "Leaky Bottom" to sea it started to speed well but in a downwards direction! They made it to Southampton but confusion arose because when they discovered that the "Speedwell" was unseaworthy they pulled into Plymouth to make repairs only to eventually abandon her and continue to America in a rather over-crowded Mayflower.

3. Plymouth Rock. It may be that the Pilgrims did step ashore somewhere where there happened to be a bit of granite but no mention was ever made of it by the Pilgrims themselves nor indeed anyone else at the time. The inference being that Plymouth Rock is only a small bolder of no historical significance.

The Arrival of the Mayflower

The Mayflower left England with about 130 passengers and crew. Most of the passengers were a mix of merchants, adventurers, servants and indentured servants (17) with only about a third being separatist puritans. They arrived off Cape Cod in November and were in a bad way. Despite previous bad experiences with newcomers the local Wampanoag Indians, led by Chief Massasoit, were responsible for saving the Mayflower Pilgrims from starvation and death during that first winter.

Even so, by March, only 47 colonists and half the crew had survived. The Colonists had two more lucky breaks. The first was that one of the Wampanoag Indians, Squanto (18) of the Patuxet tribe, spoke English. The second was that the Patuxet tribe had been wiped out by smallpox after contact with an earlier European expedition. Their now deserted village made an ideal spot for settlement. Patuxet became Plymouth.

The Wampanoag people taught the Pilgrims their farming techniques and helped them to survive in the colony. After the first successful harvest the Indians joined the Pilgrims and celebrated the "First Thanksgiving".

Chief Massasoit's Lodge (Courtesy of FCIT)

The first Thanksgiving is steeped in legend. Actually, the Pilgrims held thanksgivings quite often but they were usually days of prayer and fasting. Luckily, for future Americans, this was not the Native way. Ninety Indians arrived with turkeys for a three-day festival of eating, singing and dancing.

This peaceful co-existence was not to last. The success of the Plymouth Colony led to a Great Migration of settlers who wanted more and more of the Native Americans' land. Wars soon broke out and hostilities came to a head when Massasoit's son, Chief Metacom, led an ill-fated uprising against the settlers. The Wampanoag were nearly exterminated with only 400 surviving the war. A foretaste of what was to come.

Jamestown, Virginia

Plymouth was not the first or even most important British colony in America. Jamestown had been established some years before and was already booming. It was established by the Virginia Company. They had been tasked by King James 1 to establish a settlement in the Chesapeake area and they chose the site of what is now Jamestown. The project was beset with difficulties from the outset in the form of starvation, disease and trouble with the local Powhatan tribe. Fame and fortune eluded the settlers and investors alike.

Things changed for the better with the arrival of John Rolfe who introduced a new strain of tobacco into the colony. This became a very successful cash crop and Virginia tobacco took hold in the taverns and streets of London and then across the whole of Europe.

Relations with the local Native Americans also improved with the marriage of Rolfe and the Powhatan chief's youngest daughter Pocahontas. The Rolfes took a trip to England, where Pocahontas caused quite a stir. She was hailed as a Native American princess and was even presented at the court of Queen Anne.

Pocahontas
Courtesy of FCIT)

Tragedy befell her as, shortly after the Rolfes set sail for home, she fell ill and died. She was given a Christian burial in Gravesend. Coincidently this was just three years before the Mayflower was chartered from there and set sail on its voyage to Plymouth.

As it was so addictive, sales of tobacco were rising fast and they were already exporting tons and tons of the precious leaves. It was clear that they were going to need a lot more labour to keep up with demand for this new crop.

Harvesting Virginia Tobacco
Courtesy of FCIT)

The Slave Trade

Slavery had always been part of an empire builders tool kit. Sometimes it was limited to just conquest, oppression and servitude but the most ruthless empires went in for full-blown enslavement.

As we know, historians cannot resist using dates and they picked Jamestown, 1619 as the totemic place and date when American slavery began. As we have found before, just because something is written in a history book it does not mean that it is true. Indeed, this assignment is wrong in two particulars. Firstly, there were slaves in America long before this date (19). Second, while it is true that a British privateer, The White Lion, landed twenty captured Africans in their colony at Jamestown, Virginia in 1619 they were not sold as slaves. While there is some dispute about this there were no slave laws in place at the time and it is more likely that they were sold, just like many poor Europeans, as indentured servants (17). If the twenty captured Africans landed in Jamestown in 1619 were sold as indentured servants then, technically, they were not slaves. Indeed, two of them, Antonio and Isabella, became servants to Captain William Tucker and their son William was the first known African child to have been born in America. He was born a freeman.

Slave Auction (Courtesy of FCIT

Before anyone gets too excited by this bit of goodish news, injustice lay just around the corner. As far as black Africans were concerned, indentured servants were more often than not, forced to continue working after the end of their contract and so were effectively treated as slaves. This injustice was compounded when a Virginia court ruled that children born to enslaved mothers were the property of the mother's owner. Worse still, slavery became codified with a long list of restrictions including making it illegal to teach slaves to read. Slave codes regulated how slaves could be punished usually with no penalty for accidentally killing a slave while punishing them.

It is estimated that 12 million Africans were taken, shipped across the Atlantic and sold as slaves. Of these perhaps only 300-400 thousand were landed in America. It is a depressing fact that modern slavery (used as an umbrella term to cover forced labour, bonded debt, human trafficking and slavery-like practices) suggests that the number of slaves in present day America is a similar number ie 400 thousand (20).

The Thirteen British Colonies

The Colonies fell into three main groups:
the New England Colonies: Massachusetts, Rhode Island, Connecticut and New Hampshire. They were populated mainly by British puritans.
the Middle Colonies: New York, New Jersey, Delaware and Pennsylvania. They were mostly captured from the Dutch. They were the most ethnically and religiously diverse and very productive and became a major trade centre. the Southern Colonies: Virginia, Maryland, North Carolina, South Carolina and Georgia. These had economies based the cash crops of cotton, rice, and tobacco and had significantly higher numbers of slaves.

4 THE REVOLTING AMERICANS

The British in the American Colonies were a mean lot and they refused to pay any tax. Worse still they were cosying up to Britain's neighbours from hell, the French. This made King George mad. After all, running an army to fight the French was not cheap.

One of King George's Stamps
Courtesy of FCIT)

Now, mad King George was a keen philatelist and when he heard that the Colonists were not only refusing to pay for his stamps but they had held a "Stamp Act Congress" without asking him along, he went even madder. So he sent his army to make them pay their taxes and put a stamp on everything so he could collect them. He also closed Boston harbour because the Colonists had held a "Tea Party", again without inviting him along. Then the Colonists also became mad so everyone decided that it was the time for a Civil War.

As history is written by the winning side and spoiler alert here, the Colonists won, they renamed this Civil War the American War of Independence. This was a good thing because there were going to be two more Civil Wars and calling them by different names made American history a little less confusing that it was destined to be.

Battles of Lexington and Concord

There were many revolutionary heroes on the American side. (Note, if the British had won they would be called traitors. You see how important it is to be on the winning side when writing history). The most revered amongst them was a silversmith named Paul who, incidentally, did get an invite to the Boston Tea Party. As Henry "Wordsworth" Longfellow wrote later, Paul the Revered was the man who, legend has it, rode around shouting out "The British are coming. The British are coming."

The Ride of Paul The Revered
Courtesy of FCIT)

Now, when historians use the word "legend" what they really mean is "made up". If Paul the Revered ever said anything it would have been whispered. The Countryside was full of the British troops and pro-British Colonists. Also, Paul was himself British so he would probably have said the regulars or even the redcoats are coming but definitely not "The British are coming". Well whatever he whispered, they were indeed coming and set on destroying the Colonial military supplies stored at Concord.

It should also be mentioned that at least four others were given the same task namely Samuel Prescott, Israel Bissell, William Dawes, and even a woman Sybil Ludington. Obviously since not much rhymes with Ludington she would never appear in an epic poem. Moreover, her cry of "The British are burning Danbury!" was not nearly as catchy as Paul's "The British are coming", even if he did not actually say it. As a result, she was an early "hidden figure" (21).

To the annoyance of the British, the rebels had already removed the stores and so it was all a wasted journey except that in the various skirmishes the first shot of the war was fired. It must have made a very loud bang as it became known as "the shot heard round the world." Legend also has it that Major John Pitcairn fired the first shot using his pistols on Lexington Green. If so then Pitcairn eventually got his comeuppance in Boston but so too did the Colonists (see later). The Battles of Lexington and Concord were not that important but did force the British to bunker down by a hill in Boston where the Colonial army immediately laid siege.

The Battle of Quebec

The British strength in Canada was tested early on in the war when a small enterprising force led by Ethan Allen and Benedict "Eggs" Arnold captured a key fort. This emboldened Congress to move against the British in Quebec and General Montgomery laid siege to the city that December. Unfortunately, the enlistments of Arnold's men were expiring and as they were going home in two days' time, Montgomery was thus forced to attack. He went in under the cover of a snow storm so could climb the walls unseen. They might have gotten away with it had it not been for the lanterns the troops carried which could be seen from a mile away. While the Americans made it into the city they were easily picked off. Montgomery was killed and Arnold wounded in the failed attempt. This battle was the first major defeat for the Americans, and it came with heavy losses.

Further Colonial Defeats in Boston, New York and Philadelphia

The Colonial army had even less luck with their siege of Boston. While they captured the hill the British were bunkering down by, the British fought back and on the third attempt the Colonists, now out of ammunition, fled. Though seen as a defeat for colonial forces, the British lost a large number of men including Major John Pitcairn, of first shot fame, who was shot during the attack by Peter Salem. Salem was an ex-slave and had been given his freedom in exchange for enlisting in the provincial army.

African American Soldiers lined up; commanded by a white man.
(Courtesy of FCIT)

He was not the only black American to fight in the war. They were enticed by the offer of freedom and many black Americans enlisted on both sides and demonstrated great bravery in battle. Slave owners, including George Washington did not like the idea of brave, armed black Americans being on the loose.

British Generals Howe and Wallis (known as Cornwallis because of his bad feet) marched toward Brooklyn. Despite Washington's best efforts to keep them out, the British could not be stopped. (Well actually it wasn't Washington's best efforts as he stupidly split his forces between Brooklyn and Manhattan.) Having lost the Battle of Brooklyn the Maryland 400 held off the British while Washington and the rest of the army made a Heroic Retreat across the East River to Manhattan. They were also forced out of Manhattan and into New Jersey. Morale amongst the Colonists was dropping fast. Well if you have ever been to New Jersey you can understand why. Washington refused to engage with the British again and instead headed off to defend Philadelphia. There the British outflanked him and he made another Heroic Retreat south-wards to the alcoholically named Brandywine. Washington again committed a serious error by leaving his right flank wide open which nearly brought about his army's annihilation had it not been for several of his divisions fighting to buy him time for the rest of his army to make a further Heroic Retreat to over-winter in Valley Forge.

Battle of Saratoga

The British were on a bit of a roll and General John Burgoyne hatched a "cunning plan" with mad King George to isolate the hot bed of rebellion, New England. It was to be a three-pronged attack with one army marching south from Canada, one marching north from New York City and one marching eastward from Lake Ontario. If only the southern and western armies had arrived on time then Burgoyne would not have been surrounded at Saratoga and forced to surrender. General "Plotter" Gates's victory provided the Colonies with a much needed and first, decisive, victory over the British. While the Battle of Saratoga stopped the British isolating New England from the rest of the country, Washington's refuge in Valley Forge led to his troops suffering from harsh cold, starvation, and disease. It was not looking good and there was even a plot by Conway Cabal to replace Washington as Commander in Chief with "Plotter" Gates. Congress had two further problems. First, they were unable to challenge the British blockade on the Atlantic ports and second the attrition of their army was much greater than that of the British.

Help!

Congress soon realised that without help they could not defeat the British. The French, bitter about losing their territories to the British, wanted revenge so they joined the war. There was also no love lost between the British and the Dutch and Spanish, who were also trying to build colonial empires, so they too declared war on Britain. Passive support was also received from Russia, Norway, Denmark, and Portugal. Since America won they were able to overlook the fact that this conflict was a global war against the British and instead took full credit and called it the American War of Independence. Fair enough, the winners write the history.

Yorktown and the Treaty of Paris

Anyway, Washington now had a spring in his step and he secured a number of critical victories in the south. Cornwallis's army was left in a terrible condition so made a Heroic Retreat to the Virginian city of Yorktown. It was here that a combined French and American army led by George Washington at last defeated the British. As no side had any decent chefs left they went to Paris for dinner to discuss terms which would formally end the war. Everyone wanted peace except the Spanish who wanted war to continue until they had captured Gibraltar. The French tried to mollify the Spanish by offering them control of most of America including all the lands west of the Appalachian Mountains. The Americans realised that they would be better off cutting a deal with the British who, unlike America's so-called allies, were offering them friendlier terms. This deal paved the way to highly profitable two-way trade between the two. The British also signed separate agreements with France and Spain which all became known as the long, drawn-out Treaty of Paris.

5 THE BIRTH OF A NATION

The Magnificent Seven

There was some confusion about who was responsible for America. While the British could be blamed because they lost the war, a more positive answer was needed which included at least one American.

With great foresight, Warren G. Harding (29th President) came to the rescue just a couple of years before America became Top Nation. He invented the appellation "Founding Fathers" for those who contributed most to the Birth of a Nation. The brilliance of this rather vague definition meant that historians were free to pick their own, personal favourites and leave out those that they did not like such as Benedict "Eggs" Arnold, Aaron "Dead-shot" Burr and David Wark Griffith (22).

However, in practice, most historians usually chose the Magnificent Seven of George Washington, Alexander Hamilton, John Jay, Benjamin Franklin, John Adams, Thomas Jefferson and James Madison. To some, one of the most interesting things about the "Founding Fathers" was that Adams and Jefferson, died on the same day, the 50th anniversary of the Declaration of Independence. It must have been some party!

George Washington was the Commander in Chief of the Continental Army and famous for his many Heroic Retreats. On taking command he wrote that "it is a noble cause we are engaged in, freedom from Slavery must be the result of our conduct." The total hypocrisy of slave owners such as Washington, characterising the war of independence as a struggle for their own freedom from slavery was not lost on the British. Samuel Johnson asked "How is it that we hear the loudest yelps for liberty among the drivers of Negroes?"

Having said that, Washington (1st President) was a remarkable man. He did not want to become America's first monarch nor did he want to pass power onto his son nor did he even want to rule forever (two terms were enough for him). It is interesting to compare this with the European approach. After the French revolution Napoleon seized power, crowned himself Emperor and then had his son take over after him. It may be that Washington, unlike Napoleon, had learnt from history that despots generally come to a very sticky end. While Saint Helena was not that sticky it was certainly the end.

The Magnificent Seven
aka
George Washington,
Alexander Hamilton   John Jay   Benjamin Franklin,
John Adams   Thomas Jefferson   James Madison
(Courtesy of FCIT)

Alexander Hamilton served as the first US Secretary of the Treasury and was the first to realise that "it's the economy stupid". He set up

America's Central Bank to take over the debts of individual States and so created America's National Debt. He could have never have imagined how large this debt was going to get!

For an accountant he was a very colourful character who later starred in his own musical. He also helped Jefferson beat Aaron Burr for the presidency. Burr then ran for governor of New York State and was outraged when Hamilton said that he was unworthy to even run for a bus. A duel was fought, Hamilton was mortally wounded and Burr was charged with murder (although it never came to trial). Burr was later charged with treason and the Jefferson Administration tried hard to get a conviction. The judiciary stood firm and the Constitution's separation of powers saved the day. Well it saved Burr who then fled to Europe to escape his creditors.

John Jay was a bit of a legal eagle and became America's first Chief Justice. Not content with his part in the Treaty of Paris he wanted to have his own treaty, Jay's Treaty. This aimed to normalise relations with England so that they could all become friends again. Washington and Hamilton thought that this was a really good idea but extreme Francophile, Jefferson was against it. Naturally the French got really angry (as always). One unforeseen consequence of Jay's Treaty was that it was responsible for America's two-party political system setting Jay's pro-British Federalists against Jefferson's newly formed Democratic-Republican Party who favoured France.

Benjamin Franklin earned the title of "The First American" for his early and indefatigable campaigning for colonial unity. He was one of the five drafters of the Declaration of Independence and along with Adams and Jay negotiated the Treaty of Paris marking the end of the War of Independence.

Franklin had tried his hand at most things from making candles to editing a newspaper. Like Aristotle before him, he was very good at all kinds of sums (a polymath) but he had a playful side too and was often seen flying his kite. When kiting, in a particularly bad storm, he was shocked to discover that lightning was electrical in nature and from this key result he invented the lightning conductor to protect tall buildings.

John Adams was the first Vice-President and second President of America which made his wife Abigail the first Second Lady and the second First Lady. He was a dedicated diarist and regularly corresponded with many important figures in early American history. Adams was the primary author of the Massachusetts Constitution which greatly influenced the

Constitution of the United States.

He was the only President elected as a member of the Federalist Party. As a federalist he favoured a loose interpretation of the Constitution but a strong Federal government. He also wanted closer ties with the British and an end to the alliance with France. He also suspected that the French were aliens, from the Quasi star system. He even signed the Alien and Sedition Acts and built up America's military forces to fight an undeclared war with France which was thus known as the "Quasi-War".

Adams and his wife, Abigail produced a family of politicians and diplomats. One of their sons, John Quincy Adams, became the sixth President. They were the original Adams Family not to be confused with the Addams Family whose motto "Sic Gorgiamus Allos Subjectatos Nunc" ("We Gladly Feast on Those Who Would Subdue Us") came a close second to "In God we trust".

The Addams Family

(Courtesy of Freestock)

Thomas Jefferson was a keen supporter of the First Amendment until, when running for President, the press accused him of being a Francophile, atheist and father of six children. The number of children was not an issue it was the identity of the mother who was in fact, his slave and wife's half-sister, Sarah "Sally" Hemings. He is quoted as saying "Nothing can now be believed which is seen in a newspaper." Calling out so called "Fake News" is nothing new.

James Madison was the fourth President and co-founder of Jefferson's confusingly named Democratic-Republican Party. Madison championed republicanism, political equality, and expansionism. He also began to see the inherent hypocrisy of slave ownership. To avoid being a total hypocrite, he did release one slave, Billey (later called William Gardener), by selling him into a seven-year apprenticeship at the end of which he was freed.

The defining event of Madison's presidency was a second war with the British. This war is hardly mentioned in English history because it fell between two major battles with the French. The sea battle of Trafalgar and Napoleon's final defeat at Waterloo. These monumental British victories provided peace in Europe for the next 100 years. The war in America was thus rather trivial in comparison and in any case the British managed to keep hold of the more civilised northern territory, Canada.

The Founding Fathers and the Slavery Paradox

Adams was the only one of the Magnificent Seven who had never owned slaves and who was an abolitionist. Jay and Hamilton did own slaves but moved to the idea of manumission ie the freeing of slaves and they founded the New-York Manumission Society. Benjamin Franklin owned slaves but became an abolitionist and actively promoted education and the integration of the black population into the rest of American Society. Washington, Jefferson and Madison (except in the case of Billey) were much more politically astute about this divisive issue and were thus total hypocrites.

The Constitution

American states had been governed much like independent countries but a more cohesive federal structure was needed with rules on how government should be carried out. As usual, everybody wanted a piece of the action. Just like in ancient Rome which had Caesar, the Senate and the Generals, America had the President, Congress and the Judiciary to satisfy. The solution was to divide power three ways with the President heading up the executive branch, Congress leading the legislative branch and the Supreme Court would stay out of politics and lead the judicial branch. Well that was the plan.

We the People (Courtesy of IStock)

A Constitution was drafted which contained seven Articles. The first three detailed the separation of power between the three branches. The next three described the concepts of federalism and the relationship between state and federal governments. The seventh article established the procedure to be used by the thirteen States to ratify it.

Unfortunately, it was a bit of a rushed job and many objections were raised about who could do what to whom. To address these concerns Madison proposed ten amendments to provide specific guarantees of personal freedoms and rights and clear limitations on the government's power. Together these ten amendments were known as the Bill of Rights and owed a lot to the earlier English Bill of Rights and the much, much earlier Magna Carta.

The Second Amendment is worth a mention. It states "A well-regulated Militia, being necessary to the security of a free State, the right of the people to keep and bear Arms, shall not be infringed."

So, if you belonged to a State's Militia you had the right to bear arms. Simple. Unfortunately, the Supreme Court later ruled that the Second Amendment confers the right to keep and bear arms to everyone, however unsuited or irresponsible, not just the members of a state Militia. Oh well, at least they could get the election of a President right.

How Not to Elect a President

In fact, one of the most heated arguments over the Constitution was how to elect the President. It turned out that "one man one vote" was totally out of the question. No, not because some wanted to give women the vote. Don't be ridiculous. It was because you could not trust the great unwashed (aka the people) to pick the right person. Just imagine if they were taken in by a populist candidate offering to "clear the swamp" and actually make them President. They could also not let Congress (aka the swamp) pick the President due to the possibility, however unlikely, of skulduggery and squalid deals during the selection process.

The solution was to take it out of the hands of "the great unwashed" and "the swamp" altogether. Instead, after the popular vote each State would send independent delegates to College where they would choose the President. The number of delegates each State had was decided by size of population. As this would give slave owning States a huge advantage they made each black slave worth 3/5 of a white person.

This beautifully elegant system (aka a dog's breakfast) meant, amongst other things, that a candidate with the greatest number of popular votes could still lose the election. To date, five candidates who lost the popular vote were nonetheless elected President.

The most disastrous of these was the election of the 19th President, Rutherford B. Hayes (a bad thing). This brought an end of the Construction Era, discriminatory policies against black Americans and the imposition of the Jim Crow laws (23). A hundred years later discriminatory policies against black Americans were still prevalent in some Southern States see for example the Louisiana Literacy Test which designed to prevent black Americans voting (Appendix 2).

More recently, President George W Bush aka "Junior" (43rd President) had a run in with Al "The Internet" Bore (24) who had won the popular vote but lost the Chads who were hanging around Florida refusing to be counted.

Chads hanging out in Florida © Chandler

In the end the US Supreme Court found for "Junior" and Al went back to championing the internet, environment and all good things in general. The less said about "Junior" and his British mate Tony, the better.

Even more recently and by the largest margin yet, Hillary "The un-loved" Clinton polled 2.8 million more votes than Donald "You're Fired" Trump but she lost the Electoral College by a huge margin. The Donald became the 45th President and Hillary, "you're fired".

6 THE GREAT AMERICAN LAND GRAB

It was a bit too ironic for some Americans that thirteen ex-colonies set about colonising the rest of America so they cast the die, rolled a six and clamed it was "their manifest destiny". The river, this time the Mississippi, would be crossed.

Colonial Lands

After the War of Independence America was still surrounded by three colonial powers. The British drinking tea along the northern border, the French in control of Louisiana and the Spanish down Mexico way.

The British

Not content with having one war with the British the Americans wanted a second. With home advantage, America claimed another victory but in fact it was a score draw as the British managed to successfully defend its northern colonies. In the end they both came to an amicable agreement over the border by drawing a line along the 49th parallel. They even shared the cost of the paint.

On the other hand, America could claim to have won because the British ceased supporting the Native Americans in their fight against American expansion in the West. So, while Britain and America could both claim to have won, the Native Americans definitely lost.

The French

War with the French was also looking increasingly likely. Well they were the French after all. However, on the advice of a French friend, Jefferson offered to purchase land from Napoleon. Now, Napoleon, because of his war with the British, was strapped for cash, so he offered the entire Louisiana territory at a bargain basement price of less than three cents an acre. Jefferson's Francophilia had paid off.

The Spanish

The Spanish were far less friendly and claimed that Florida and the southern lands were all theirs. They eventually did do a deal and gave Florida to America as long as they kept their hands-off Texas. Meanwhile America was about to get a new neighbour.

Mexican Lands

When Napoleon occupied Spain, Mexico had their own War of Independence. It was started with the cry of "Grito de Dolores". No one knows who Dolores was but she obviously made great grits. As a result, thousands of grit loving natives and mixed-race, Mestizos flocked to join a peasant army. Mexico was free and they even abolished slavery.

However, one region of Mexico, Texas, had invited a lot of Americans (with their slaves) to settle there. The new regime soon became a threat to their way of life and so they too decided to revolt. Unfortunately, Texas could only muster a small army so their commander, Sam Houston, set off to recruit more men. He left behind two small forces one at the Alamo and the other at Goliad.

Mexico's President/General Santa Anna went on the attack. This Santa was far from a benevolent present giver. He was a cruel man with despotic tendencies (a bad thing). The legendary attack on the Alamo left most of the small garrison dead. This included the famous hatter, Jim Crocket and singer, David Bowie. Santa Anna did however, let surviving non-combatants and slaves leave. This included Joe, the slave of the Alamo's commander William Travis. Joe fought alongside his master but after Travis's death hid in the chapel and so was assumed to be a non-combatant. After his release Joe was again enslaved for being black but escaped back to the Travis plantation where he told his story of the Alamo. No one knows what happened to Joe but his heroism was never rewarded.

A worse fate lay in store for the small force outside Goliad who were overwhelmed by the Mexicans and forced to surrender. Just in case people thought that Santa Anna was going a bit soft, he ordered all 400 Texans, who had been taken prisoner, to be executed.

Houston now had a force of 800 men and on hearing the news of their dead comrades set upon Santa Anna's much larger army shouting "Remember the Alamo!" and "Remember Goliad!". The fight lasted just 18 minutes, Santa Anna fled and Texas became America's 28th State. Foolishly, Mexico then started a war with America. They not only lost the war but also even more territory extending westward from the Rio Grande to the Pacific Ocean. If only they had built a wall instead.

Westward Expansion

The white Americans attacked the Native Americans on three fronts: disease, war and Andrew "Jackass" Jackson (7th President) (25).

Europeans were a disease-ridden lot and while they themselves had some immunity to smallpox, influenza and measles, the Native Americans did not and so half of them died. In order to justify the taking of Indian lands the white settlers had invented "Manifest Destiny". The problem was that the Indians did not know what that meant either so they created the "Indian Problem".

Washington (1st President) thought that the best way to solve the "Indian Problem" was to make Native Americans as much like white Americans as possible. ie convert them to Christianity, teach them English and get them to adopt European practices such as personal ownership of land, property and of course, African slaves.

The Cherokee, one of the "five civilized tribes"
(Courtesy of FCIT)

The Cherokee tried this approach but Andrew "Jackass" Jackson stopped his usual practice of vetoing bills and passed the Indian Removal Act. This was the only major bill he passed in his two terms of office. Now the Cherokee had indeed adopted many European practices and so their John Ross took legal action. Even though several court rulings found the Cherokee to be the rightful owners of land, these weren't enforced mainly because even if you walk like, talk like and sue like a white American the Cherokees were still just "Indians". Defeated, Ross was forced to lead his people on a brutal march to Oklahoma. The neighbouring Creeks suffered the same fate and many died on what became known as the "Trail of Tears."

It was the same everywhere. About 100,000 Native Americans living between Michigan and Florida were moved west onto Government Reservations. Various Treaties were signed which provided money and rights to the Native Americans but were invariably broken. The phrase "speak with a forked tongue" was certainly applicable to the actions of Government officials. Hollywood, of course, not only made the Indians the baddies but also made them sound stupid by missing out the "a". "Indian say white man speak with forked tongue" became the catch phrase of western movies. With or without the "a" it was not the white man's finest hour.

Here we have to pause the American-Indian war as Americans decided to have their own Civil War.

7 THE AMERICAN CIVIL WAR

Things had been going very well for the newly formed United States of America so it was now time for a civil war. Remember, there had not been one yet as the Americans had beaten the British and so, as winners, called it a War of Independence.

Now, you could argue that there was already a civil war in progress. Hostilities between the Native Americans and the white American settlers had been going on for some time. However, it was decided that since Native Americans were in fact Indians (even though they did not play cricket) this war should be known as the American-Indian War. It was not at all civil.

The North–South Divide

The industrialising North and plantation-based economy of the South were growing far apart. Although both needed labour the North was benefiting from newly arriving migrants while the South still relied on slaves, at least four million of them. There was also an increasingly vocal abolitionist movement and a belief, in the South, that the Federal Government was hell bent on taking decisions about slavery away from individual States. The scene was thus set for conflict and all that was needed was a catalyst.

Enter stage right, the newly elected, first Republican, President, Abraham Lincoln. Exit stage left, South Carolina, Mississippi, Florida, Alabama, Georgia, Louisiana, and Texas now called the Confederation of American States under their very own pro-slavery, president, Jefferson Davis.

Even though Lincoln thought that secession from the Union was illegal he did his level best to calm things down. In his inaugural address he declared that he had no lawful right to interfere with the institution of slavery and that he would not start a Civil War with the South. Lincoln was that rare breed of leader who had learnt a little bit from history and that Civil Wars were a Bad Thing.

Despite these clear and unambiguous pledges war broke out. Even back then, Americans didn't believe what Presidents said nor trust Federal Government.

The Abolitionist Movement

At the beginning of the 19th Century the abolitionist movement stirred. The British banned the Atlantic slave trade altogether. Many in the North became concerned for the oppressed black population of the South even though most had no idea how these slaves lived day-to-day. A cunning plan was hatched to show Northerners how wonderful slavery really was. Music hall introduced white entertainers who blacked up their faces and sang and danced and had a jolly good time of it helping out their friendly Masters. These blackface entertainers grew in popularity and one of the most popular was T D Rice and his black persona Jim Crow (22). Strangely, as the popularity of these minstrel shows increased so did the growth of the abolitionist movement and another "best laid plan" went wrong.

Speaking of rubbish plans, lets take a ferry to coincidence-ville. Some abolitionists were inclined to speed things up a bit and take direct, violent action. One such person was John Brown of "lies a-mouldering in the grave" fame. Intent on initiating a slaves revolt he planned an attack on the Arsenal at Harpers Ferry to get hold of the arms. Meeting strong resistance he and his band took refuge inside one of the Arsenal buildings. Guess who was in overall command of the force to retake the arsenal. None other than Robert E. Lee. Later, Lee's army pals, Stonewall Jackson and Jeb Stuart, were part of the troops guarding the arrested Brown and none other than Lincoln's assassin, John Wilkes Booth, was a spectator at Browns execution. So, the first Confederate victory over the abolitionists took place some two years before the Civil War began!

A Far from "Civil" War

This was America's most costly war. It lasted four years and claimed more lives than any other American conflict, an estimated 750,000 men (26).

The first major battle was just 30 miles from Washington at Bull Run. The Union side were clear favourites to win and so, of course they lost. This turned out to be a blessing in disguise as the Union side realised that maybe they should train their soldiers and appoint commanders who knew something about military tactics and how to fight.

There were at least 50 major battles during the war but the double burger of them all were the battles at Vicksburg and Gettysburg. They, were the turning point in favour of the Union.

At Vicksburg, the Union forces were under the command of General Ulysses S. Grant. To pick someone called Ulysses (Greek Odysseus) for a siege was, of course, inspirational. At least someone in Washington must have read Homer. While it is not known if a wooden horse was involved, the Confederate army surrendered giving the Union the ability to cross the Mississippi any time they wanted and without even having to roll a six.

Meanwhile at Gettysburg Robert E Lee was trying to invade the North and came up against General Meade's Union army. Holding the Union flank was George Armstrong Custer and the Michigan cavalry. Custer was a bit of a peacock and took great pride in his appearance, especially his cascading golden locks, which he perfumed with cinnamon oil. Known as "Custard" to his English friends, he had finished last in his class at West Point. However, he was the swash and buckle kind of officer and rose rapidly through the ranks.

General Custard and his Golden Locks
(Courtesy of FCIT)

With battle lines drawn a key objective was control of the aptly named Cemetery Ridge. Lee sent his infantry to take the Ridge while his cavalry, led by Jeb Stuart, attacked Meade's flank. Custard held firm and Lee beaten and bruised made a Heroic Retreat back down South. Why Meade did not follow Lee and finish him off remains a mystery. The rumour in the Sergeant's mess was that Meade had picked Appomattox in the army sweepstake on where Lee would finally surrender.

The Era of Reconstruction

After the Civil War the United States set about building bridges between the North and South and to begin the painful process of reintegrating the defeated Confederate States back into the Union.

President Lincoln belonged to the school of thought that the freed black population should be given full rights as American citizens including male suffrage (after all they were good at suffering). There was also a Klan of thought that the ex-slaves should do all the building work and if they had to be free then they should keep themselves to themselves.

Well, things got off to a very bad start. It happened at Ford's Theatre when an actor named John Wilkes Booth entered stage left, went completely off-script and shot and mortally wounded Lincoln. Vice President Andrew Johnson took over who, unlike Lincoln, was a Southerner, a former slave owner and thought that what individual States did with the ex-slaves was no business of Federal Government. The bridge building was off and reconciliation between white and black Americans was not going to happen any time soon. Outbreaks of violence against the black population in the former rebel states and even the massacres of ex-slaves went un-punished.

Republicans eventually got back into power enabling them to pass the 14th Amendment, federalising equal rights for freedmen. Northerners flocked south to help out and were called "old bags" after their cheap luggage. As the luggage was often made of old carpet they were also known derogatively as "shag piles".

The next elected president was Republican Ulysses S. Grant (18th President) who supported Reconstruction and enforced the protection of African Americans in the South through the use of the Enforcement Acts backed up by US troops. He also set upon the Ku Klux Klan, which was essentially wiped out although not gone forever. Nevertheless, Grant was unable to resolve the escalating tensions and support for Reconstruction waned as taxes rose.

Four years later, the "How not to elect a President" protocol demonstrated how bad things could get. The result for the election of the 19th President had Democratic candidate Samuel Tilden win the popular vote and although nineteen votes ahead of his rival in the Electoral College was still one vote short of the number needed to win the election. A further 20 College votes were in dispute due to issues of corruption, intimidation and eligibility so, according to the Constitution, Congress had to resolve the issue. They set up a commission who, after a backroom deal, awarded all 20 votes to Rutherford B. Hayes giving him the Presidency by one college vote.

Rutherford B. Hayes - A bad President
(Courtesy of FCIT)

So, what was this squalid deal? Well, in return for the Presidency, Republicans agreed to remove all Federal troops from the South, which opened the doors for discriminatory policies against black Americans and the imposition of the Jim Crow laws (23). It was the end of the Era of Reconstruction and for the black population a disaster "whose magnitude cannot be obscured by the genuine accomplishments that did endure" (27). Such discrimination would never be far away. Even 100 years later the so called "literacy tests" were being used to deprive black Americans of their voting rights (Appendix 2).

8 THE "WILD, WILD WEST" SHOW

The American Indian wars - Continued

After the Civil War the army was able to get back to the American-Indian war. Remember, this was not a civil war because Native Americans were Indians.

The US government had very generously given all Native Americans reservations at Best Westerns but as these had not yet been built, they had to rough it outside on the open plains. They were not happy and were in a rebellious mood. As night follows day, civil unrest follows injustice. Death and destruction rained down upon settlers and properties across the West were razed to the ground.

In response, the government sent in the SS (Sheridan and Sherman) to provide a solution to the "Indian Problem". Fortunately, it was not the final solution. Now, both men liked playing with matches and had been responsible for the Union's scorched earth policy during the Civil War. Sheridan devastated the Shenandoah Valley while Sherman burnt his way through plantation after plantation as he marched through Georgia. While it was Sheridan who had infamously said "The only good Indian is a dead Indian", they were both fully signed up to "Total War" where there was no differentiation between combatants and non-combatants, including women and children. The SS double act made Santa Anna look like an old softie.

Ever since Gettysburg, Sheridan had been a fan of Colonel Custard so he invited him to take command of the famous 7th Cavalry. Custard's first mission under Sheridan's winter offensive was to attack the Cheyenne in their village on the Washita river. They attacked from four directions at once killing their Chief, Black Kettle, and many others. Meanwhile, warriors from nearby villages began to gather and Custard, seizing the women and children of the village, used them as a human shield to make a rapid but Heroic Retreat. During the battle a small group of troupers led by Major Joel Elliot got separated. Custard's Heroic Retreat without trying to help his missing men, did not go down well with Elliot's best friend a certain Captain Benteen.

Although the stakes were stacked against the Native Americans they refused to go quietly and some of their great leaders became legends in their own lifetimes. One such figure was Geronimo who led the Chiricahua tribe of the Apache. He led many attacks on both Mexican and American settlers and was one of the most exciting and feared Indians of the period. This combination of excitement and fear is, of course, the reason why people yell his name when jumping out of airplanes while hoping their parachute will open. In his later years he sold autographs and posed for celebrity selfies with paying customers! A few years before he died, at aged 80, he was at the World's Fair in St. Louis where he is said to have ridden a Ferris Wheel.

Another Apache Chief and one of the last holdouts in resisting white settlement, was Cochise. Panicked settlers abandoned their homes, as the Apache raids took hundreds of lives and caused huge damage to property. Anxious for peace, the government offered Cochise a huge reservation in the south eastern corner of Arizona Territory if they would cease hostilities. Cochise agreed and checked in.

Red Cloud was one of the most important leaders of the Lakota and one of the most capable Native American opponents that the United States Army faced. The largest action of the war was the Fetterman Fight in which 81 U.S soldiers were killed. This was the worst military defeat suffered by the United States Army on the Great Plains until the Battle of the Little Bighorn.

The A-Team Right a Wrong

Sitting Bull was Chief of the Sioux and one of the most respected chiefs in the last years of Native American struggle. He was the spiritual leader of the tribes that united against the US Army. After the American-Indian Wars he became a celebrity and appeared in Buffalo Bill's Wild West Show.

Crazy Horse, a Lakota warrior, was considered to be the greatest American cavalry leader of all time. He amassed more than 1,200 warriors to help Sitting Bull defeat General Crook and after that, Sitting Bull and Crazy Horse joined forces and became the A-team.

The Native American's A Team Sitting Bull and Crazy Horse
(Courtesy of FCIT)

The Battle of the Little Big Horn

The Native Americans called it "The Battle of the Greasy Grass" but as the US won the American-Indian Wars they got to name it as "The Battle of the Little Bighorn". It also became known, rather solidly, as Custard's last stand.

Before the battle, information had reached Custard that there were only 800 "hostiles" and his scouts had also located Sitting Bull's village. Custard threw caution to the wind and attacked immediately. Splitting his force in three, he and Reno attacked from two sides while the third detachment under Benteen held back as back-up in case back-up was needed.

Reno met strong resistance at the village and his men had to dig in. Custard and his 220 men, ran into at least 2,000 Sioux and Cheyenne warriors. Hearing the gunfire Benteen went to help and with the cry of

"Remember the Washita" rushed to Reno's aid. The rest is, as they say, history.

Well two histories, depending upon who you believe. On the one hand the heroic General Custard under attack by the Indian hoards and left unsupported by his drunken/incompetent officers Reno and Benteen, fought bravely to the last man. On the other, Custard was his usual impetuous self who, without knowledge of the enemy strength or position, divided his small force and gifted the Indians their well, deserved victory.

The Indian Wars Come to an End

Unfortunately for the Native Americans, news of the massacre of General Custard and his 7th Cavalry made white Americans incandescent with rage and government troops flooded the area forcing the Native Americans to surrender. The Indian War came to an end.

There were many more injustices inflicted on the Native Americans over the following decades. They were not even recognised as American citizens until just after America became Top Nation. Even then not all were allowed to vote.

How the West Was Really Won

Western expansion into what became known as the American Frontier had given rise to many tales of hardship, toil and strife. However, a novelist named Zane Grey and an aspiring actor named "Buffalo Bill" were responsible for re-branding this rather dusty affair into tales of derring-do and created the Legendary Wild West.

"Buffalo Bill" whose real name was William F. Cody, started out as a solicitor's clerk from Iowa. He loved amateur dramatics but could never get into the parts of all the Western characters he tried to play. Coming across a book on method acting showed him the way. He had to become those characters. So off he set to do just that. He took part in California's Gold Rush, worked as a Pony Express Rider, an army scout in the Indian Wars and fought on the side of the Union in the Civil War. By the time he was ready to launch his acting career he was already a real-life Western legend. His new found fame allowed him to star in his own wild, Wild West Show. To add some realism to his show he recruited many Plains Indians as extras. He also recruited the great Sitting Bull.

His two female leads were Calamitous Jane and Annie "Get Your Gun"

Oakley. Calamitous Jane was an adventurous frontiersman. Perhaps it should be frontierswoman but Calamitous was famous for dressing (and drinking) like a man. She was, however, definitely a woman and even had a crush on Buffalo Bill. In fact, it was her drinking that gave rise to her name and people kept her well away from their best china. Annie Oakley was a real-life sharpshooter who, at only 15, competed and beat an expert marksman who she also married. As Buffalo Bill's female stars they met royalty and world leaders.

The Wild West Show Goes On
(Courtesy of IStock)

To act in and direct his show he chose Wild Bill Hitchcock. He was known for telling outlandish tales about his adventures often keeping people in suspense and on the edge of their seats. He too took on many jobs out West and was a wagon master, lawman, gunslinger and gambler and became one of the most famous folk heroes of the era. His end came when shot in the back while playing poker in Deadwood. Legend has it that he was purportedly holding two pairs of black aces and eights, now known as the "dead man's hand".

During Buffalo Bill's highly successful tour of his Wild West Show, Zane Grey's adventure novels took off and "Riders of the Purple Sage" became his best-selling book. Hollywood recognised the potential of this new genre so invented the Western and Grey's best seller was an early adaptation onto the silver screen and released as "Purple Rain". It made a princely sum at the box office.

9 AMERICA BECOMES TOP NATION

America had blossomed during the Victorian era and was looking forward to an even better new century ahead.

Meanwhile, the Europeans had been building yet more Empires. In fact, there were three more: the Austro-Hungarian, the German and the Italian. As ever, there was trouble brewing in the Balkans who wanted to be free from these wretched empire builders and have their own independent Yugoslavia. If only they could get rid of the Austro-Hungarians.

It so happened that Archduke Franz Ferdinand, heir to the Austro-Hungarian throne, was visiting Serbia to review the Imperial troops. He was driving along in an open carriage with his wife Sophie when shots rang out and they were both mortally wounded. The Austro-Hungarians, especially Emperor Franz Josef, were somewhat miffed.

Meanwhile, Kaiser Bill, the diminutive Emperor of Germany's 2nd Reich, saw an opportunity to move up the league table of empires. He had already been building up Germany's military and was ready to play with his new toys. He had even bought a new helmet, with a spike sticking out the top, so that he would be as tall as everybody else.

He pledged his support to Franz Josef who he then persuaded to declare war on Serbia. Since Russia supported the Serbs, Germany declared war on Russia and as France supported Russia, Germany and France declared war on each other. (You really could not make this stuff up!) War began when Germany marched through neutral Belgium to attack France. The British felt obliged to join in due to the probability of a German invasion when France inevitably gave up.

The Kaiser's Helmet Extension
(Courtesy of GoGraph)

The biggest surprise about all this war mongering was that no-one thought about what a fully mechanised war would look like nor how long and deadly it would be. Everyone really did think that it was going to be done and dusted by Christmas and that the Tsar and Kaiser would then be invited for tea at Windsor.

America wanted nothing to do with this and kept well out of it. Indeed, Woodrow Wilson was re-elected as President on an anti-war ticket. Fortunately for the British, Germany made two fundamental mistakes. First, they embarked on unrestricted submarine warfare to isolate British supply lines. The German High command knew that, by sinking American merchantmen, they risked America entering the war so they sent a secret telegram to Mexico offering an alliance which would see Germany help Mexico recover Texas, Arizona, and New Mexico. British intelligence loved intercepting and decoding secret messages and passed it on to Washington. An angry America declared war on Germany. As we know, Germany was beaten, English history ended and America became Top Nation. What could possibly go wrong?

Party Time

Well actually, it all got off to a rollicking good start. America decided it was time for change so made everyone use automobiles, telephones and all sorts of electrical appliances. Aviation took off. The West saw rapid industrial and economic growth. American Culture was invented (a bad thing). In true American style, it all began with a huge, very noisy, party. In fact, it was so noisy that people had to shout to be heard which is why this decade became known as the "Roaring Twenties".

Runnin' Wild with the Charleston
(Courtesy of GoGraph

It was also the time when many democracies gave women the vote. A good/bad thing, delete as appropriate. Note that both options are included for completeness but the publisher will not be liable for what happens to any man caught crossing out the word "good". Of course, some men were driven to drink by all this suffrage especially when women refused their help to put the cross in the right box. In a somewhat over-reaction to this the Government introduced prohibition (a bad thing).

The banning of alcohol meant that crime had to be organised to make and supply illegal alcohol so that the party could continue. Gin was the easiest spirit to make but vermouth was in short supply, which is why American martinis are made mostly of gin.

It was actually very easy for people to continue to drink during prohibition. Herbert Hoover (31st President) just popped into the nearest foreign embassy for his daily, quite legal, tipple. Ordinary folk had to sneak into one of the many illegal speakeasies but most found that breaking the law added an extra frisson to a night out. It also saw the popularity of jazz grow with the resultant increase in both inter-racial mingling and the acceptance of women in bars. Due to the threat of raids, finger-food came into being so people could make their escape and take dinner with them.

Of course, all good things must come to an end and in the morning after all this partying everyone had a really bad hangover and felt very, very depressed. It turned out that all the money had gone, there were no jobs and people were now having a thoroughly rotten time of it. It became known as the "Great Depression".

Never Again!
(Courtesy of GoGraph

On the positive side it was the start of "The Golden Age of Hollywood" (a good thing). Hollywood had invented "talking pictures" ie ones where the actors speak rather than just mime the words. These new "talkies" provided much needed escapism from real life.

Franklin D. Roosevelt (FDR) for President

Depression began to be lifted following the landslide victory of Franklin D. Roosevelt (32nd President) who promised people a "New Deal". FDR also introduced the concept of "the first 100 days" in office on which all Presidents are now judged. The first hundred days are essentially a President's honeymoon period when he or she can get things done before party politics grinds government to an acrimonious halt. No President has yet beaten FDR's record. He managed to reform fiscal and monetary policy, banking, securities and most importantly, he repealed prohibition, all within 100 days.

World War 2

The Great War was supposed to be the war to end all wars but when the Allied powers met in Versailles (on the outskirts of Paris) to draw up the peace treaty there was complete disagreement. Wilson (28th President) had a conciliatory approach but the French wanted to cripple Germany once and for all and because Versailles was in France they got their way (always a bad thing). The British PM, Lloyd "Nostradamus" George, thought the treaty too harsh and even said "We shall have to fight another war again in 25 years time." While it probably did not cause the second world war it did give A Dolf a perfect excuse for some of his initial actions from which war was inevitable.

It soon became clear that the Germans had the upper hand with a new, diabolical, secret weapon, the "Blitzkrieg". They deployed their "Blitzkrieg" and country after country fell. The French were however not worried as they were hiding safely behind their Ligne Maginot (Magic Line). Just in case it was magic, the dastardly Hun aka Germans went around the back through the muddy field called Belgium. Taken by surprise, the French immediately threw down their weapons and changed their name to Vichy France (a bad thing). Now the British had sent an extraordinary force to help out but with the fall of France they beat a Heroic Retreat back to Dunkirk. As the ferries were no longer running, they had to be picked up by a cobbled together armada of hundreds of small craft. Because the evacuation had been organized by Churchill himself it was lauded as a major success and gave England a huge boost to moral.

Even though America was now Top Nation, FDR did not want to get dragged into another bloody European war. With Europe defeated the British now stood alone. FDR was sympathetic and stretched America's neutrality and supplied military hardware on a lease-lend basis. He and Churchill had many a telephone conversation that always ended with Winnie signing off with KBO (Keep Buggering On). And by George they did!

Meanwhile Japan, Germany's ally, had been picking fights with everyone in the Far East and while negotiating peace with the US they sneaked up on Pearl Harbour to sink America's Pacific Fleet. America entered the war.

Initial hostilities in Europe began with the GI invasion of England. GIs were reportedly very generous. With average salaries more than five times that of a British soldier there was plenty of time for parties. GIs were frequently described as "overpaid, oversexed and over here". The GIs retorted and said the British were "underpaid, undersexed and under Eisenhower" Touché! In the end, around 70,000 British women actually became GI brides. A much needed boost to British exports.

After the Allied defeat of Germany, it became clear that America had a rival for the Top Nation slot namely Russia. Russia was led by a ruthlessly, nasty individual named Stalin. He was not even a corporal so the army gave him their newly invented, highest rank of Generalissimus. This was for two reasons. First, they could not take orders from a private and second because Stalin had a short fuse and they all valued their privates.

Do not go on holiday with Uncle Joe!
(Courtesy of GoGraph

To try and make post war relationships work FDR, Stalin and Churchill went on holiday together to the resort city of Yalta. It was one of those holidays that you want to forget. There was certainly a chill wind blowing from the East.

10 BABY IT'S COLD OUTSIDE!

Communism

Americans like a party but they drew the line at the Communist Party and self-elected, party-pooper in chief, Joseph "Red under the bed" McCarthy would stop at nothing to prevent America falling into their hands. No-one, however innocent, was safe from his attention and like all zealots, McCarthy did not understand the meaning of the word restraint.

Project Fear!
(Courtesy of GoGraph

The extremes of McCarthyism did come to an end but America's obsession with Communism led to wars with Communists in Korea and Vietnam. But it was its old war-time ally, Russia, that caused the most trouble.

The American Dream

Most people can't remember their dreams but Americans can. Actually, it is always the same one. You arrive in New York by sea with only the cloths you stand up in. You get a great welcome and if you are lucky, even a de-lousing and then sent off to make your fortune. You work hard and soon have a House, a Buick, a wife/husband and two point four children. But then it goes nuclear. Yes, these were nuclear families because Russia (The Great Bore) is making lots of nukes and pointing them westward. In return, America built lots of their own and pointed them back at Russia. Each side also installed a nuclear button so that mutual destruction could be assured.

Fortunately, neither side fired any of them so the planet didn't go up in a ball of flame (well mushroom) and since global warming had not then been invented this was called the Cold War. A bad thing.

Note: it was George Orwell that first used the term "Cold War" but Shakespeare had also foretold our winter of discontent and no doubt Nostradamus had said something, somewhere about someone catching a cold at some time.

The Space Race

To make matters worse Russia launched a Sputnik into space. This was a small metal ball with four antenna that made a very annoying beeping sound as it went around the Earth. The Americans were furious as all this beeping was keeping them awake so, by jiminy, they were going to do the same but even better.

Sputnik Started It!
(Courtesy of GoGraph)

Then the Russians ramped things up and sent a dog into orbit. That was it and America rushed to get their own big rocket off the ground and.............it blew up! Oh well, back to the drawing board and Russia had won the first heat. They also won the second when they put a Yuri into orbit and returned him safely to Earth.

This was too much for John F Kennedy (35th President) as to win the race he would have to get a whole baseball team into orbit. Instead, he cleverly changed the rules to whoever puts the first man on the moon is the overall winner. This time America did win. Neil Armstrong stepped out onto the surface of the moon and messed up his lines. "One small step for man one giant leap for mankind" should have been "One small step for a man one giant leap for mankind". Note that as no women had been involved in this historic space program except the "Hidden Figures", who were indeed well hidden, so Armstrong's message about man was quite correct.

Hollywood takes Over and breaks the Ice

The cold war was dragging on and not only was it costing lots of money but both the Russian and American leaders were tired of keeping their finger hovering over the nuclear button.

Just one push away from nuclear Armageddon
(Courtesy of GoGraph)

Things got even worse when Jimmy "Peanuts" Carter (39th President) became president. His main achievement in office was to give away the Panama canal but he also ramped up the pressure on those hovering digits by banning grain exports to Russia.

Fortunately, the election of actor Ronald Regan (40th President) brought a breath of fresh, warm air into east-west relations. Regan was also a bit of a wag and poked fun at "Peanuts" by explaining that "A recession is when a neighbour loses his job. A depression is when you lose yours. And recovery is when Jimmy Carter loses his." On age he noted that Thomas Jefferson once said, "We should never judge a president by his age, only by his works. And ever since he told me that, I stopped worrying."

Perhaps that was why he got on so well with the Russian leader Mikhail "Glasnost" Gorbachev (8th and last President of the Soviet Union). "Glasnost" (openness) brought "perestroika" (restructuring) to Russia which led to the end of the Cold War, the fall of the Berlin Wall and freedom of the countries of the Eastern block. Russia became a shadow of its former self, albeit a rather sinister shadow.

11 AMERICA GOES DIGITAL BUT IT'S THE END OF THE DINER

For Whom the Bell Tolls it tolls for......Analogue.

Although America is known for its cracked bell (see "The Philadelphia Story") there was a Bell in New Jersey that was far from cracked. Bell Labs was at the centre of another American revolution which gave rise to the digital age. Now digital usually means counting up to ten using your fingers but Bell Labs produced a device where you only needed two fingers. In fact, you didn't actually need any fingers at all because the hard work could now be done with a transistor. This new, binary system became all the rage and numerous companies formed to exploit the opportunities this new Tech made possible. As with Washington before them, these Tech companies did not fancy New Jersey and so set up in California instead. They settled in a very sandy hollow, Silicon Valley, where they multiplied. You could do a lot more with a transistor than just add. They also made special chips out of all that sand.

An ingot of pure Silicon ready for the chip pan © Chandler

There are two types of Tech company, those that make things e.g. phones and computers and those that do not make anything. They make their money out of being purely digital. Now making money from nothing is okay if you can pull it off but some of them were a bit like snake oil sellers and when they tried to inflate a digital bubble it burst and they fell by the wayside. The ones that remain went from strength to strength to monopoly. Two key players are Dumpling Inc. and Macrohard who set up in Seattle because they heard that something was brewing there. Dumpling Inc. make phones and computers which are beautifully engineered but designed to become obsolete as soon as you switch them on. They thus make huge profits from selling the next, soon to be obsolete, "must have" models. Macrohard make software that is so full of bugs that it has to be regularly up-graded which provides huge, on-going revenue streams. Interestingly, they both developed their products having seen the brilliant Doug Engelbart's "Mother of all Demos" (28) which gave them the basis for their future technical success.

Outside America, an Englishman named Sir Tim (29) was busy inventing the Web which like all empires was to be built on the back of Cerfs (30). Sir Tim was an unashamed geek and thought that his Web was pretty cool and wanted everyone to have a share in it. Unfortunately, at first, no-one apart from Ted Nelson (31) seemed to know what the hell to do with it. In fact, it was one of those strange inventions that until you start using it you can't possibly imagine what it is capable of. It turned out that it was to completely change the world. One group that benefited were a group of tech companies including Facebook (in England known as Clegg-book), Twitter, Instagram and a few others. They got together to form the "Social Network". Actually, all they did was provide the platforms and it was the people who created the whole thing. Well that is what the wife keeps banging on about anyway (32).

Unfortunately, all this success went to the Tech companies' collective heads when they started to realise that all the information being shared by people on their machines and "Social Network" was very valuable. Not only could it help sponsors target people with products they did not want or need and could be rapidly bought by pressing the wrong button, but that they also became the modern day "Big Brother" (a bad thing). This particularly negative part of American history is far from over.

Alas poor diner

One tragic consequence of the digital revolution was the decline of the great American Diner. These fabulous restaurants provided Americans all across the Country with their favourite food throughout the day. While the food might not have been gastronomic it could be washed down with unlimited supplies of weak, rather lukewarm coffee. Customers could while away the hours with their all-day breakfast and read USA Today from cover to cover.

The Great American Diner (top) Gave Grounds to Coffee (Work) Houses (bottom) (Courtesy of GoGraph)

Unfortunately, a company called Starmuck invented real coffee. Based out of Seattle they soon spread everywhere giving Americans a much needed, shot (or three) in the arm. Also, with all these digital gadgets and "Social Network" there was just no time to either eat a meal or read USA Today. All people wanted was to be kept awake with lots of real coffee and to connect to their digital world. So, Coffee Houses were in and Diners were gone (a bad thing).

12 AMERICA THE DECLINING YEARS

As we saw in Chapter 2, Empires rise up, decline and fall and then their history then comes to a full stop. While America may not have quite reached this point it is clearly the beginning of the end. This is for two main reasons, the effects of globalisation and running out of money.

Globalisation

When Columbus discovered America, people began to realise that the world was not flat and so they had to invent Globalisation. The British were the first to go Global and built the British Empire over which the sun never set. In time, with the introduction of fast ships and aeroplanes, the world got a lot smaller (this would have really pleased Columbus) and companies became global as well. They soon realised that if they moved their production to these now not so faraway places they could take advantage of really cheap labour.

Business goes Global (Courtesy of GoGraph)

So, people in China were paid a pittance to do the work previously carried out by expensive American labour. This meant nice cheap products for the consumer and nice big profits for American companies. A win-win?

Well, in one sense, it was actually a step back to the time of indentured servants, a bad thing. It also gave rise to two problems. First, Americans lost their jobs because the "slaves" now had them. Second, in order to enable the poorer countries to make things, they had to be given access to American technology. While China might have been a poor country to begin with they were far from stupid and soon not only mastered these technologies but improved upon them and then invented their own. China became the clear winner of Globalisation.

The American Dream Ran out of Money.

While building an Empire can be a lot of fun (well for the builders rather than the people who do all the heavy lifting) there comes a time when they simply run out of steam and cash. America got a bit carried away will all that building and they are now finding out how much it costs a lot to keep it from crumbling away. Americans had also been on a huge spending spree.

A run on the Dollar?
(Courtesy of GoGraph)

While an Englishman's home is his castle an American's home is where they keep their stuff while they are out buying more stuff. To put it bluntly, their credit cards were maxed out. To add insult to injury, as the American

Dream ran out of money the gap between rich and poor widened. America should have sorted out its excessive borrowing as well as issues such as racial tension and adequate provision of health care during the good times. (Easy to say now but historians have always been blessed with 20-20 hindsight).

Quo Vadis America?

While it is pretty obvious that American history is approaching its own full stop (or period, to make them feel a bit happier about it) it does provide an opportunity for Americans to re-boot their democracy, civil rights and the American Dream. More importantly, they could even bring back the great American Diner. In the meantime, there is always karaoke! Sinatra anyone?

And now, the end is near
And so I face the final curtain
My friend, I'll say it clear
I'll state my case, of which I'm certain

I've lived a life that's full
I travelled each and every highway
And more, much more than this
We did it the American way

13 THE EPILOGUE

Space-time distortion aside, it is difficult to write history, memorable or otherwise, before events have actually happened. Nevertheless, change, like the Corona virus, is in the air and probably from the same source. If only the West had taken Napoleon's advice, "China is a sleeping giant. Let her sleep, for when she wakes she will move the world."

China has been the clear winner of Globalisation and everyone else is hugely in her debt, literally. The development of strong economic, technical and military platforms makes China well placed to take over and is already flexing their muscle and influence around the world. The recent annexation of Hong Kong and the sabre rattling in the South China sea do not bode well for their near neighbours especially ones they claim are theirs anyway. So, unless somebody can come up with a better idea, it looks like the world really will be dominated by a powerful, dictatorial, expansionist, Chinese Empire (a bad thing). Well who else is there to take over as Top Nation? The self-important and totally delusional European Union will obviously fancy themselves in the role and no doubt have a roadmap already worked out. The main problem is that this un-democratic, putative State was already in decline even before Brexit.

But wait! What about giving democracy another chance? When the British lost their empire, they became quite good friends with their ex-colonies. They joined together as equals in a Commonwealth of Democratic Nations. The 54 members include four of the World's five eyes. The fifth eye, the USA, is not a member but as 13 of the 50 States were once a British Colony letting them all join should not be a problem if they wanted to. Other democratic Nations like Japan could also join. Well why not for goodness sake (a very pleasant drink when warmed). So China, if/when you become Top Nation, please be nice to everyone or you might see a re-make of the "Empire Strikes Back"!

对人好点 "Be Nice"

APPENDICES

Appendix1 Notes

Appendix 2 Louisiana State Literacy Test

Appendix 3 The Forbidden Zone

APPENDIX 1 NOTES

1. "1066 and All That: A Memorable History of England" W. C. Sellar and R. J. Yeatman published by Methuen & Co. Ltd. 1930.

2. America is used throughout to mean any and all lands that became the modern United States of America. This is because we are not allowed to call them the Colonies anymore.

3. The Dominique Calendar is a simple ruse used to avoid any preferential treatment given to one religion over another.

4. The Meadowcroft Rockshelter is an archaeological site located near Avella in Jefferson Township, Washington County, Pennsylvania, United States. The site is a rock shelter in a bluff overlooking Cross Creek, and contains evidence that the area may have been continually inhabited for more than 19,000 years

5. Santayana, The Life of Reason,1905. (Often confused with Carlos Santana).

6. Actually, only one gibbon., Edward Gibbon, who wrote "The Decline and Fall of the Roman Empire". Coincidentally the first volume was published in 1776 and the last (sixth volume) was published a few years later at the start of the French Revolution. No causal link has yet been established.

7. If you ever wondered how we are able to read hieroglyphics; it Is down to the discovery of a lump of granite built into the wall of a fort near the northern Egyptian town of Rashid (Rosetta). It was found by Napoleon but then confiscated by the ever present British. It now resides in the British museum in London. The Rosetta Stone features a decree written in three ways: in hieroglyphics, in ancient Egyptian demotic and in ancient Greek. Scholars were able to crack the code and read what the Egyptians had written all over their walls – even the very rude bits.

8. Antony and Cleopatra, Coriolanus, Julius Caesar and Titus Andronicus

9. Dipped candles were one of the many things that the Romans did for us (see "The Life of Brian"). They were made from rendered animal fat or tallow.

10. A cricketing expression describing the difficulties of playing on a very damp, soft pitch. The British were certainly up against it and the sea off Trafalgar was indeed very damp. Like Drake before him, Nelson was indeed a fine bowler.

11. Source www.jewishvirtuallibrary.org

12. Brexit. The British Exit from the EU.

13. Suzerainty Treaty. A relation between states in which a subservient nation (the UK) has its own government, but is unable to take international action independent of the superior state (the EU).

14. Terry Pratchett's Discworld is a comic fantasy about a flat world held up by four elephants all balanced on the back of a giant turtle. Don't tell anyone but he may have stolen this idea from the Hindus (15).

15. "Hindu Earth". In Hindu mythology, earth is supported by four elephants standing on the back of a turtle.

16. "The Vicar of Bray" is a satirical song about a Vicar fundamentally changing his principles in order to retain his ecclesiastic office.

17. Indentured servants. In the case of white Europeans, they had agreed to work with no pay for a set amount of time before being freed from their contract.

18. Squanto. The local Indian tribes belonged to the Wampanoag grouping. They had already had contact with English explorers who had captured some of them and taken them away to England. One such man was named Squanto of the Patuxet tribe. In England he lived with Sir Ferdinando Gorges, who was Governor of Plymouth and keen promoter of colonisation in America. Sir Ferdinando taught Squanto English and hoped to use him as interpreter/guide in further explorations of the West Coast region. Indeed, Squanto returned to his homeland but was captured once again by another British expedition and this time sold as a slave in Spain. He managed to escape back to England and once again returned to his homeland only to find that his whole village had been wiped out by smallpox. Squanto was the last of the Patuxets.

19. The Spanish brought slaves to their colony in St Augustine where they were used to build a fort long before 1619.

20. Global Slavery Index.

21. As history has been traditionally written by men the focus was naturally always on what other men did. The occasional Queen was, of course, worth a mention but generally women were kept very much in the background or completely written out of history. Hence the term "hidden" figures.

22. David Wark Griffith. Pioneer film maker whose highly successful but controversial silent film "Birth of a Nation" both exposed and promoted racism in America.

23. Jim Crow. The name of this character was used to describe a

collection of statutes that legalised racial segregation. The "Jim Crow Laws".

24. Al "Internet" Gore (AG) was given a lot of stick for allegedly claiming to have invented the Internet. The real pioneers of the Internet, Vinton Cerf and Robert Kahn came to his defence and confirmed the help he had provided to promote and support this wonderful invention.

25. Andrew "Jackass" Jackson was the founder of the Democratic Party and that is why all Democrats are known as Jackasses. Strangely, the Republicans who disliked Jackson began to wear Whigs. It was a passing trend.

26. Findings of demographic historian Prof. J. David Hacker published in the December 2011 issue of Civil War History.

27. A disaster "whose magnitude cannot be obscured by the genuine accomplishments that did endure". Historian Eric Foner.

28. Doug Engelbart's "Mother of all Demos" demonstrated a working prototype of linked computers, windows and a mouse, way before these products were developed.

29. Sir Tim Berners Lee Inventor of the World Wide Web and responsible for all that http and html stuff that changed the world.

30. Should of course be "serfs" but Vinton Cerf is recognised as one of "the fathers of the Internet" without which the Web could not operate.

31. Ted Nelson pioneer of information technology, philosopher and sociologist.

32. Dame Wendy Hall Executive Director of the Web Science Institute at the University of Southampton. Giving her a mention in the book also gets me lots of brownie points!

APPENDIX 2 THE STATE OF LOUISIANA LITERACY TEST

The Literacy Test was, in effect, a way to prevent black Americans voting. It had 30 confusing questions which had to be completed within in 10 minutes. Ten examples are reproduced below. One wrong answer meant a fail and thus no right to vote.

Draw a line from circle 2 to circle 5 that will pass below circle 2 and above circle 4.

Draw a line around the shortest word in this line.

Look at the line of numbers below, and place on the blank the number that should come next.

3   6   9   __   15

Circle the first, first letter of the alphabet in this line.

Spell backwards forwards.

Print a word that looks the same whether it is printed frontwards or backwards.

Write every other word in this first line and print every third word in same line, but capitalize the fifth word that you write.

Draw five circles that one common inter-locking part.

In the space below draw three circles one inside (engulfed by) the other.

Divide a vertical line in two equal parts by bisecting it with a curved horizontal line that is only straight at its spot bisection of the vertical.

APPENDIX 3 THE FORBIDDEN ZONE (GENUINE DATES)

As some strange people actually like dates (go figure) the following list has is made to make them happy. The rest of you can cut along the dotted line and move this page to a suitable receptacle.

The two Genuine Dates used in "1066 and all that" were 55 BC the start of English history and 1066 for William the Conqueror.

The three extra Genuine Dates used here are 1492, when American history began, 1619 when American slavery began (although it did not) and 1776 the Declaration of Independence.

Dates of the 5 Bad Presidents
1829   Andrew "Jackass" Jackson (7th President).
1862   Jefferson Davis (1st President of the Confederate States).
1865   Andrew Johnson (17th President).
1969   Richard "Watergate" Nixon (37th President).
2001   George W Bush "Junior" (43rd President).

The, three American Civil Wars but only one is recognised by Americans.

1609 - 1924 The American-Indian Wars. This was deemed not to be a Civil War because Native Americans were in fact Indians even though they did not know where India was nor how to play cricket.
1775 -1783 The War of Independence. Again, this was not a Civil War between the revolting British Colonists and the British Government because the Colonists won and became Americans. Nor was it a World War against the British because Americans wanted to take all the credit.
1861 - 1865 The American Civil War ie the only approved Civil War.

Four Other Genuine Dates

1620 Mayflower sets sail from Southampton not Plymouth.
1812 Another war with the British which the Native Americans lost.
1861 The first telegraph message sent across America ie Internet 0.
1918 English history ends and America becomes Top Nation.

ABOUT THE AUTHOR

The author is a Physicist who, in his teens, was given a copy of the wonderful "1066 and all that" by his father. If only school history lessons had been as free of dates and half as much fun as the book he may have become an historian. Perhaps any Americans who have read this book will be very happy that he did not!

ADDENDUM

Although history repeats itself it is rarely perfectly timed hence the horribleness of dates. The title of this book should, of course, have been "1766 and all that" to provide a nice number of hundreds after the original 1066. Furthermore, it also ruins the pattern for future Memorable Histories namely "1866 and all that, a Memorable History of the European Union" and "1966 and all that, a Memorable History of China".

Americans must take the blame for this. King George repealed his hated Stamp Tax in 1766 and had the Colonists been less revolting the "66" series could have been unblemished and the bookshelf a much more ordered place (a Good Thing).